My First NFL Book

DENVER BRONCOS

Nate Cohn

LET'S READ
AV²
BY WEIGL™
ADDED VALUE • AUDIO VISUAL

Go to **www.av2books.com**, and enter this book's unique code.

BOOK CODE

X742794

AV² by Weigl brings you media enhanced books that support active learning.

AV² provides enriched content that supplements and complements this book. Weigl's AV² books strive to create inspired learning and engage young minds in a total learning experience.

Your AV² Media Enhanced books come alive with...

Audio
Listen to sections of the book read aloud.

Video
Watch informative video clips.

Embedded Weblinks
Gain additional information for research.

Try This!
Complete activities and hands-on experiments.

Key Words
Study vocabulary, and complete a matching word activity.

Quizzes
Test your knowledge.

Slide Show
View images and captions, and prepare a presentation.

... and much, much more!

Published by AV² by Weigl
350 5th Avenue, 59th Floor
New York, NY 10118

Website: www.av2books.com

Library of Congress Control Number: 2017930544

ISBN 978-1-4896-5502-8 (hardcover)
ISBN 978-1-4896-5504-2 (multi-user eBook)

Printed in the United States of America in Brainerd, Minnesota
1 2 3 4 5 6 7 8 9 0 21 20 19 18 17

032017
020317

Editor: Katie Gillespie
Art Director: Terry Paulhus

Weigl acknowledges Getty Images and iStock as the primary image suppliers for this title.

My First NFL Book

DENVER BRONCOS

CONTENTS

The Denver Broncos started playing football in 1960. The team almost moved to another state in 1965. That is when brothers Gerald and Allan Phipps stepped in. They bought the Broncos and kept them in Denver. The team joined the NFL five years later.

Excited fans started buying three times as many tickets after the team was saved.

5

The Stadium

The name of the Broncos' stadium is Sports Authority Field at Mile High. The fans there make loud noises they call "thunder." They make thunder in the upper deck by stomping on the steel floor. This is one way that fans cheer on the team.

A big horse statue called Bucky towers over Sports Authority Field at Mile High in Denver, Colorado.

Team Spirit

The Broncos have two horse mascots. One is named Miles. This is because Denver is called the "Mile-High City." The second is a real horse called Thunder. His name comes from the city's many thunderstorms.

Thunder runs from one end zone to the other after each Broncos touchdown.

The Jerseys

The team's first jerseys were brown and gold. The Broncos' colors are now orange and blue. They usually wear orange jerseys with blue stripes for home games. The Broncos have also worn blue jerseys with orange stripes. The team wears white shirts on the road.

The Helmet

The Broncos' helmets are blue with the team logo on both sides. The Broncos' logo is a white horse with an orange mane. The helmets also have an orange stripe down the middle. The stripe ends in a point before reaching the facemask.

An older logo had a horse with the letter "D" for "Denver."

The Coach

Vance Joseph was named the Broncos' head coach in 2017. This former NFL cornerback is known for being smart about defensive plays. This is Joseph's first job as a head coach. He worked with the defenses of several other NFL teams before joining the Broncos.

Player Positions

Defensive tackles are large players that line up against the offense. Teams have one or two of these players on the field at a time. Defensive tackles try to push through the line to get to the ball. They will often spin their arms or "swim" past blocks.

There are about 100 tackles in each NFL game.

Star Player

Von Miller is a Broncos linebacker. He has gone to the Pro Bowl five times since 2011. The Pro Bowl is played by the NFL's best players each year. Miller forced two fumbles during the 2015 season's Super Bowl. A fumble happens when a player drops the ball. Miller was named that game's Most Valuable Player.

John Elway was the Broncos' quarterback for 16 seasons. He was known for his heroic plays late in games. Elway won two Super Bowls. He was named the NFL's Most Valuable Player in 1987. Elway is now the team's general manager. He is in the Pro Football Hall of Fame.

Team Records

The Broncos first made it to a playoff game in 1977. The team has been in 22 NFL playoffs total. The Broncos have gone on to win three Super Bowls. Wide receiver Rod Smith made 849 receptions in his career. Smith's total is a team record.

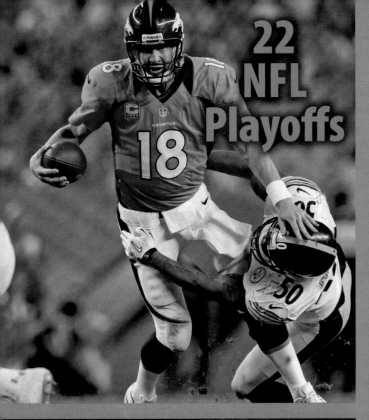

22 NFL Playoffs

3 Super Bowl Wins

Rod Smith

849 Career Receptions

By the Numbers

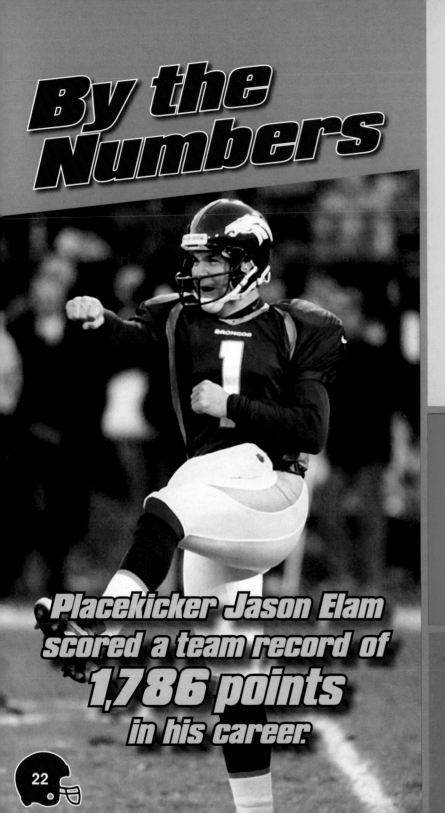

Placekicker Jason Elam scored a team record of **1,786 points** in his career.

There are more than **63,000 people** on the waiting list for Broncos' season tickets.

John Elway made **300** touchdown passes. His career total is the **10th highest** in the NFL.

The Bucky statue is **27 feet tall**.

Running back Terrell Davis rushed a team record of **7,607 yards.**

The Broncos have been to **8 Super Bowls.** Only one team has been to more.

Quiz

1. How do Broncos fans create "thunder"?

2. What is the name of the Broncos' real horse?

3. How many fumbles did Von Miller force at the team's last Super Bowl win?

4. For how many seasons was John Elway the team's quarterback?

5. How many Super Bowls have the Broncos won?

ANSWERS 1. By stomping their feet on the steel floor 2. Thunder 3. Two 4. 16 5. Three